Plans to Prosper:
Strategies, Systems & Tools Workbook

By: Victoria Cook & Stan Washington

Plans to Prosper: Strategies, Systems, and Tools Workbook

.

Printed in the United States of America

First Printing, 2010

ISBN: 978-0-9909831-4-9

DEDICATION

This book is dedicated to small businesses who are driven to make the world a better place with their innovation.

CONTENTS

ACKNOWLEDGMENTS

Thanks to the thousands of the small businesses, startups, and entrepreneurs who allowed us to serve you over the years and were open about your business needs.

FIRST 30 DAYS—READINESS PHASE

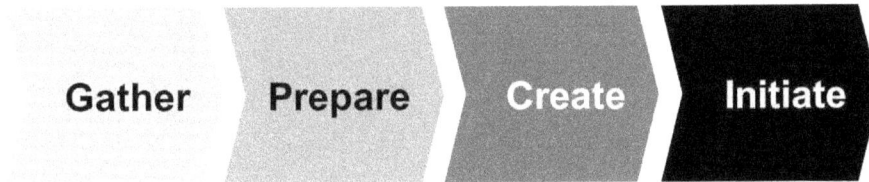

Gather   Prepare   Create   Initiate

GATHER

After completing the exercises in the readiness phase, you will have a detailed understanding of your market and their needs. This will ensure that you have chosen a viable customer base and understand where to find them. It also ensures that your marketing aligns your solution to their problems.

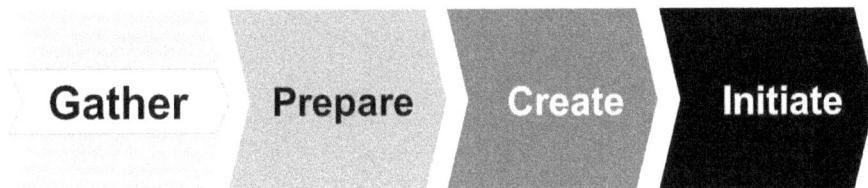

In the gather phase, you will enter your competitive analysis information. This should be done with a large enough sample to understand pricing, service and offerings of your competitor. We have provided you common questions you can use to build your own analysis of your market.

Knowing your market is extremely important so be wary of breezing over this exercise too quickly. Fill in as much information about your market as possible.

Instructions:

1. Make copies of the Market Survey pages and use these to complete your competitive analysis.
2. Make copies of the Know Your Market pages and use these to complete your customer and product analysis.
3. Once you have collected your information, write your conclusions and use this as input to your plan in the Prepare phase.

MARKET SURVEY

It is important to understand what your competitors are doing and what they are saying about their product and compare it to yours. You can then identify how your product or service fits into the marketplace and how to differentiate it from your competition. (**See Pages 15 - 19 - Plans to Prosper: Strategies, Systems and Tools for Small Business Marketing Success paperback book**)

COMPETITOR ANALYSIS

Company Name: _____

Product or Service Name: _____

Description of what I offer: _____

_____

_____

_____

Product Pricing: _____

Annual Sales in Dollars (if available): _____

Customer Purchase Frequency: _____

Competitor	Similar Product/Service	Competitor Price	Product/Service Features

How my product/service compares to the competition:

_____

_____

_____

Ways my product/service stands out from the competition:

_____

_____

_____

COMPETITOR TRAFFIC ANALYSIS

Conduct a traffic analysis to record the traffic outside a brick-and-mortar storefront. Record information in military time to avoid confusion. Remember to count cars from both rush hours (6:30—9:30 a.m. and 4:30—7:30 p.m. aka 16:30—19:30).

Record counts **in 15-minute increments** using tick marks. Repeat the study for the opposite direction. For Example: **8:00 - 8:15**   ‖‖ (This old fashion way is easiest and cost effective).

Time in Military Time	Number of Cars

KNOW YOUR MARKET

What specific market or segment of the market is your product/service geared toward? Being specific about your market will help you market effectively, draw your market toward you, and position your offering as a solution to the problems they face. (**See Pages 20 - 22 - Plans to Prosper: Strategies, Systems and Tools for Small Business Marketing Success paperback book**)

CUSTOMER PROFILE

Market segment or client category: _____

Problem / Challenge / Experience my market is seeking: _____

_____

_____

_____

Ideal Customer:

    Average Age: _____

    Gender: _____

    Marital Status: _____

    Location or Area: _____

    Income: _____

    Education Level: _____

    Home Owner: _____

    Other demographic information of importance: _____

_____

_____

Motives for purchasing my product/service: _____

_____

_____

Reasons current customers have made their purchase: _____

_____

_____

My top 5-10 customers have the following in common: _____

_____

_____

_____

_____

_____

My ideal market looks for solutions to their problems in the following locations:

1.

2.

3.

4.

5.

    6.

    7.

    8.

    9.

    10.

The words and feelings my ideal clients use to describe the problem they have and solutions they seek are:

_____

_____

_____

_____

Top Five Challenges/Problems my Ideal Customer Faces:

    1.

    2.

    3.

    4.

    5.

The products/services I can offer my ideal market that solves these challenges/problems are:

    1.

    2.

    3.

4.

5.

What positive feelings or emotions does your product or service evoke?

_____

_____

Does your product or service cost more or less or the same as your competitor?

_____

_____

Is the quality higher, lower or the same as competitor?

_____

_____

CORE MARKETING MESSAGE

Use the action verbs and the words used by your ideal clients to describe your product or service and how it will resolve their issues.

_____

_____

_____

_____

_____

GATHER CONCLUSIONS

What price(s) will I set my product(s) or service(s) at now that I have completed my competitive analysis?

What changes to my product or service should I make?

How can I leverage my competitor analysis to reach my target market?

PREPARE

After completing this step, you will have a clear vision and plan that provides focus and easy implementation for a higher success rate.

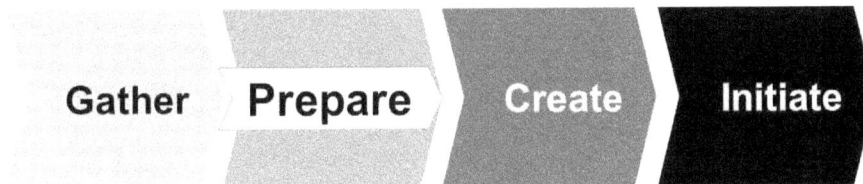

Gather   **Prepare**   Create   Initiate

In the Prepare phase, you will set your goals and build your plan leveraging the Market Survey and Knowing your Market information. Discuss your goals and your plans with other trustworthy people at the right time.

Instructions:

1. Fill in the Setting the Course pages and use these to complete your goals.
2. Fill in the Marketing Plan pages and use these to complete your detailed plan.
3. Once you have collected your information, write your conclusions and use this as input to your plan in the Create phase.

SETTING THE COURSE

My SMARTER (Specific, Measurable, Achievable, Rewarding, Time-Based, Evaluated & Revised) values-based goals for the next: (**See Pages 24 - 26 - Plans to Prosper: Strategies, Systems and Tools for Small Business Marketing Success paperback book**)

Month:

    1.

    2.

    3.

Quarter:

    1.

    2.

    3.

    4.

    5.

Year:

    1.

    2.

    3.

    4.

    5.

What measures will you put in place for these goals? _____

_____

_____

_____

How will you achieve this goal(s)? _____

_____

_____

_____

How are your goals relevant to your customer's needs? _____

_____

_____

_____

What date(s) will you evaluate the effectiveness of your marketing goals? (Remember to add this date to your calendar)

_____

_____

How will you "Magnetize" your goals? (Tie to a cause, your purpose, values, a business need or respect in the market place are a few examples.)

_____

_____

_____

MARKETING PLAN

It's tempting for business owners to start their business, open the doors, and jump into business ownership. But upfront planning will save a lot of time, money, and frustration. This is a living document that you will want to regularly update and refine throughout the entire High-Achieving Marketing Process™. (**See Pages 27 - 33 - Plans to Prosper: Strategies, Systems and Tools for Small Business Marketing Success paperback book**)

Business Name	
Goals	
Ideal Market *(The ideal clients who will most benefit from what I offer & are willing to pay for it.)*	
Top 5 Challenges of My Market	1. 2. 3. 4. 5.
Service/Product Offered *(A suite of products or services working together to solve your customers' core problem(s))*	

Core Message *(Top three messages that will resonate most with my ideal market segment or client and the problem I solve.)*	1. 2. 3.
Killer Elevator Speech *(A seven- to thirteen-word statement that distills the essence of what you do, for whom, and the benefit they will receive from your service or product.)*	
Tag Line *(A positioning statement or a promise of how customers will experience or feel about the product or service.)*	
My Unique Process *(The unique way in which I work with clients and help them achieve their success.)*	
Pricing Strategy / Packaged Deals *(Pricing and introductory programs or packages to helps solve the problems of my market.)*	Introductory Price: Bundled Pricing: Pricing Tiers: Low, Medium (Most Attractive), High

Risk Reversal *(What can I do to eliminate the financial risk for my market & help them say yes to buying from me?)*	
Why Choose Me? *(Why my market should choose me over the competition.)*	
Connection Points *(Places I can find my market congregating in person or online)*	
My Marketing Channels *(The top 3-5 marketing channels that will best meet my market.)*	1. 2. 3. 4. 5.
Content Strategy *(What content can I offer my market that will be beneficial, position me as an expert, and attract them to my business?)*	

Marketing Strategies *(The specific marketing strategies I will use to attract, acquire, and retain my ideal market.)*	**Attraction Strategies:** **Acquisition Strategies:** **Retention Strategies:**
Marketing Tactics *(The specific methods I will use to promote my goods or services.)*	

Marketing Budget	**Last Year's Revenue:** **Current Cash Flow:**
Tools *(The business tools I will use in my business)*	Business Cards Packets of Information Trifold Flyer Website Postcards Booth Banner (Sign)
Tracking *(The key metrics I will track to determine the ROI of my marketing time and investment in strategies and tactics.)*	

PREPARE CONCLUSIONS

What barriers to my SMARTER goals can I expect and how should I adjust my plan?

What changes to my budget should I make now that I have completed my marketing plan?

How can I leverage my competitor analysis and target market information to adjust my plan?

CREATE

After completing this step, you will have a clear vision of how your market perceives your brand. You will also have actions to add to your calendar to drive your plan.

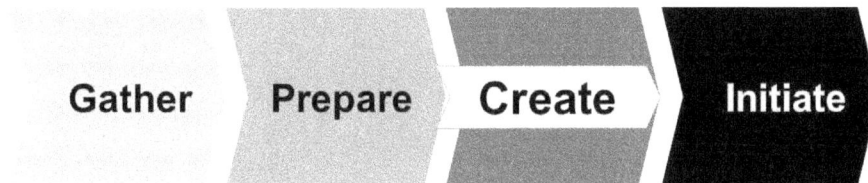

Gather   Prepare   Create   Initiate

In the Create phase, you will build or modify your brand and set specific dates to execute your plan leveraging the Market Plan and SMARTER Goal information. Determine if you need assistance from professionals.

Instructions:

1. Fill in of the Branding pages and use these to modify or establish your brand.
2. Fill in specific dates as to when you will execute your marketing.
3. Once you have collected your information, write your conclusions and use this as input to the Initiate phase.

BRANDING

BUILDING YOUR BRAND - (SEE PAGES 35 - 38 - PLANS TO PROSPER: STRATEGIES, SYSTEMS AND TOOLS FOR SMALL BUSINESS MARKETING SUCCESS PAPERBACK BOOK)

Naming your Company, Product or Service

What is the name of my company, product or service?

_____

_____

Does the name have meaning or is it catchy and memorable?

_____

_____

Is the name short enough? Can I go with an alias?

_____

_____

Is the name available?

_____

_____

How do I wish for my business to be recognized? (Descriptive or Emotional Response or Whimsical) – See Chapter on Branding

_____

_____

Is Trademarking my name to protect my brand needed?

_____

_____

Logo

Does this name need a logo or icon? _____

How will I use the logo? (Stationary, Website, Facebook, LinkedIn, Twitter)

_____

_____

What shape logo will I choose? _____

_____

The keywords that represent my brand are: _____

_____

_____

BANNER (WEB PRESENCE)

Resources I will use for developing my banners (Fiverr, DIY, or Hire a Graphic Artist):

_____

_____

Have I developed a Banner for my:

Website

LinkedIn

Facebook

Twitter:

MARKETING CALENDAR

(See Page 39 - 42 - Plans to Prosper: Strategies, Systems and Tools for Small Business Marketing Success paperback book)

Marketing Calendar	Daily:
(A specific plan of what I will do each day, week, month, quarter and year that implements my tactics and strategies and achieves my business goals.) *See the Creating Your Marketing Calendar in the Plans to Prosper book.*	**Weekly:** **Quarterly:** **Annually:**

Schedule time on your calendar to take specific actions outlined in your plan and marketing calendar and keep them like appointments with your best client.

CREATE CONCLUSIONS

Have I included my mission and values into my Brand?

What professional do I know who can develop professional looking banners and pictures.?

How can I leverage my Marketing Calendar to adjust my plan?

INITIATE

After completing this step, you will move past excuses that have led to marketing avoidance in the past. You will be pumped to proceed while ensuring you have the time to get everything done.

Gather **Prepare** **Create** **Initiate**

In the Initiate phase, you will examine barriers to completing your marketing goal. Time management is key to executing your plan so we provided you with a process to follow while overcoming marketing obstacles.

Instructions:

1. Fill in of the Marketing Guilt pages to overcome barriers.
2. Fill in Time Management plan to ensure you accomplish your goal. Use your Marketing Calendar and Marketing Plan as input to this process.
3. Outsource some of your processes to look more professional. Fill in the areas you will leverage a professional.
4. Once you have collected your information, write your conclusions and use this as input to the Second 30 Days (Execution Phase).

GOT MARKETING GUILT?

(See Pages 44 - 48 - Plans to Prosper: Strategies, Systems and Tools for Small Business Marketing Success paperback book)
Feeling guilty about the amount of time you are spending on your business, charging for your services, or what you believe you may need to do to market your business? Guilt can hold you back from achieving the goals you have set. That's why it's important to overcome it.

Overcoming guilt starts with identify its source: lack of a clear vision and plan; unreasonable expectations and standards; or a lack of confidence about what you offer and how you help your clients.

The source of my guilt is: _____

_____

_____

Providing my product or service to customers is important to me beyond the financial aspect because:

_____

_____

_____

WHERE DOES THE TIME GO?

(See Pages 49 - 54 - Plans to Prosper: Strategies, Systems and Tools for Small Business Marketing Success paperback book)

Many of us know that the world is not in our control, but there *is* one thing we *can* control: our behavior. We choose what to do in our business, either by intention or by default. This is the key to time management.

Allocate time for the important components of running and marketing your business. A good rule of thumb is 40% of your time on product/service delivery, 35% on marketing, 15% on networking and offsite meetings, and 10% on administrative work.

Track how you spend your business time for one week. This can be done simply with pencil and paper, or if you prefer a digital option, Paymo.biz is a free online tool that is easy to use for time tracking.

In order to better manage your time and marketing, you may need to say "No" to some things. Trouble saying no and suffering from calendar clutter? Saying no is not rude; it doesn't mean you aren't a team player or that you are being selfish. Learning to say no is a learned skill. It can be difficult to do, but it is valuable to achieving and maintaining balance in life and creating the time needed to work on your marketing.

Saying no is about choosing: choosing to say yes to those things that are profitable and productive to your business and bring you greater energy, or allow you to utilize your talents, while saying no to the things that suck the life from you or step on your values. You must choose and you must know what you have chosen by making a deliberate and conscious decision.

Sometimes saying "No" is the best thing you can do for yourself and the requestor. Remember, you want to say "Yes" to those things that increase your energy and sense of fulfillment, and that capitalize on your natural abilities, talents, and passions.

Follow these three steps to Guilt-Free No's:

1. Recognize that when you say Yes to one thing you are automatically saying No to something else.

2. Buy yourself time to avoid "reactive yes's". Tell the requester you need to think about it or consult others. Make it a habit to wait 24 hours before providing answers, even to small requests.

3. Then say Yes, No or give a Counter Offer.

    •   YES: A Yes can be a straight out Yes or a conditional "Yes, if..."

        "Yes I can help you on Tuesday if I can leave by 2 pm."

    •   COUNTER OFFER: Give a Counter Offer for what it is you can agree to do.

        "I can't meet with you on Tuesday but would have time on Wednesday morning if that works for you."

    •   NO: When a no is needed, use a No Sandwich. A No Sandwich takes the no (often thought of as the "negative part") and sandwiches it between two positive statements affirming the requestor or the relationship.

"Thanks so much for the invitation to your networking event. It sounds like a great event for business owners. I won't be able to make it, but I hope it goes well. You're such a terrific networker and your guests will surely have a productive time."

Notice there isn't an excuse included. It's not really necessary. When No is said using a No Sandwich, both you and the requester can still feel good about it despite any disappointment on either side.

Remember, you don't have to say NO to everything, just ensure you are saying Yes to the RIGHT things for empowering reasons.

Use No's to clear some of the calendar clutter to make room for the things that give you energy physically, emotionally, and spiritually (daily/weekly/monthly and are important for you to complete.)

I will say No to: _____

_____

_____

My business hours are:

- Sunday:

- Monday:

- Tuesday:

- Wednesday:

- Thursday:

- Friday:

- Saturday:

OUTSOURCING MARKETING

(See Pages 55 - 57 - Plans to Prosper: Strategies, Systems and Tools for Small Business Marketing Success paperback book)

What parts of your Marketing Plan can I pay for to maximize that strategy?

_____

_____

What questions will I ask to assess the marketing company?

    For Example:

        What connections to large groups do you have?

        What "Partnering" strategy do you propose?

        What is the Content Marketing Strategy?

        What is the PR Strategy?

        What is your email Marketing Strategy?

        How will they handle advertising?

        What is you policy on Social Media Outsourcing?

_____

_____

_____

INITIATE CONCLUSIONS

What adjustments to my Marketing Plan will I make, knowing what barriers I have identified?

What Time Management adjustments can I make to my overall plan?

What Outsourcing decisions have I made that will change my overall Marketing Plan?

FIRST 30 DAYS IMPLEMENTATION CHECKLIST

GATHER

- ☐ Read the introduction and the First 30 Days section to get an overview.

- ☐ Create a physical folder or digital folder for all notes and materials.

- ☐ Put time on your calendar each week to work through the process.

- ☐ Conduct initial market research.

- ☐ Identify your first ideal market segment.

- ☐ Find the top 10 locations from which your ideal market segment gains information.

- ☐ Draft the top five challenges the ideal market faces

- ☐ Begin a draft of your market survey.

- ☐ Create a spreadsheet of top competitors.

- ☐ Research competition and those with whom you directly and indirectly compete.

- ☐ Finalize and complete market survey.

- ☐ Draft a product mix or list of service offerings of interest to your ideal market.

PREPARE

- ☐ Draft SMARTER goals.

- ☐ Review market research and survey results.

- ☐ Begin a draft marketing plan.

- ☐ Write out values, short mission statement, or elevator pitch for your business in 40 words or less.

CREATE

- ☐ Review and finalize the top five challenges your ideal market has for which you have resources.

- ☐ Refine product mix/service offering based on market research and survey results.

- ☐ Review marketing survey data and ensure the marketing messages address the core concerns of your market.

- ☐ Identify keywords that represent your brand.

- ☐ Decide on a logo or font treatment for your business.

- ☐ Finalize logo or font treatment.

- ☐ Identify two or three social media sites to connect with your audience.

- ☐ Draft a marketing calendar of what tasks to be done daily, weekly, and monthly.

INITIATE

- ☐ Start time log to track time use.

- ☐ Set core business hours.

- ☐ Identify and eliminate marketing guilt.

- ☐ Identify what tasks can be outsourced now and in the future.

- ☐ List in a document why serving clients is important to you.

SECOND 30 DAYS—EXECUTION PHASE

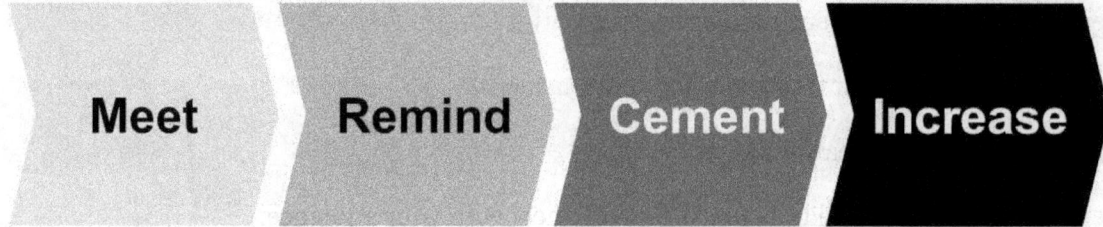

Meet   Remind   Cement   Increase

MEET

After this step, you will have engaged the audience and proven your expertise.

In the Meet phase, you will build or modify your list of people and places you will build your contact list. develop your elevator speech, grand opening plan and content marketing genre.

Instructions:

1. Fill in of the Marketing While Networking pages and use these to modify or establish your Elevator Speech.
2. Fill in your Grand Opening Plan (use this to Launch New Products or Services).
3. Determine how you will be seen as the expert through Content Marketing.
4. Once you have collected your information, write your conclusions and use this as input to the Remind phase.

MARKETING WHILE NETWORKING

(See Pages 64 - 69 - Plans to Prosper: Strategies, Systems and Tools for Small Business Marketing Success paperback book)

Top 3 – 5 places I can network and meet my prospects, potential power partners and peers are:

_____

_____

_____

_____

_____

How many meaningful relationships do I have within my network?

_____

_____

_____

After networking events I will use the following steps to follow-up and make the most of my time spent:

1.

2.

3.

4.

5.

6.

7.

My Killer Elevator Speech that answers the question, "What do you do?" when networking is:

_____

_____

The tools I will use when networking are (examples include business cards, flyers, copy of latest newsletter, postcards, etc.)

_____

_____

Use a Customer Relationship Management (CRM) tool, like Honor Services Office, to track new prospects. Things to consider tracking include when you meet, how many times you have spoken to them, and future contact dates.

I will track the following things for each new contact and prospect:

_____

_____

OPEN FOR BUSINESS

Grand Opening

Whether you are opening the doors of a brand-new business, launching a product, or offering a new release, hosting an event or a grand opening is a terrific way to let your network and community know about your business, and create some buzz. **(See Page 70 -73 - Plans to Prosper: Strategies, Systems and Tools for Small Business Marketing Success paperback book)**

The date of my Grand Opening is: _____

Type of event I will host (in person, virtual, ribbon cutting, open house, mixer, launch party, etc.)

_____

_____

Type of connections I want to make at this event include (e.g. current or past clients, prospects, media, power partners, etc.)

_____

_____

Ways I will announce my event include:

_____

_____

Marketing strategies I will use to promote my event are:

_____

_____

_____

_____

The message that will resonate most with my prospects and clients and promote my event is:

_____

_____

High level plan of tasks to complete for this event are:

1.

2.

3.

4.

5.

6.

7.

8.

9.

10.

Offer or Special I can offer during my event is: _____

_____

_____

My multi-step follow-up plan for after the event to help move prospects one step closer to buying from me are:

1.

2.

3.

4.

5.

6.

7.

8.

9.

10.

CONTENT MARKETING

(See Pages 74 - 77 - Plans to Prosper: Strategies, Systems and Tools for Small Business Marketing Success paperback book)
Audiences are becoming more and more sophisticated. They want more information than "here is my product, buy it." A good strategy for marketing is to focus on the top 5 -10 problems or challenges your market faces and why it is important to them to resolve them. This will provide you with content marketing topics that will be of interest to them and on which you can share solutions that will help.

The top five problems of your ideal market are:

1.

2.

3.

4.

5.

What kind of information can I share with my market that addresses their challenges and positions me as an expert that can help solve their problem.

_____

_____

_____

_____

_____

In what way is my market looking to receive the information I have to share? E.g. Videos, white paper, news interviews, ebook, short tips, etc.

_____

_____

Where does my market go to find solutions to their problems? E.g. Magazines, white pages, other referral sources, newspaper, etc.

_____

_____

_____

_____

My areas of expertise are:

_____

_____

Can I tell a story and make my content a journey?

What new concepts can I illustrate or explain that would be of benefit to my market?

_____

_____

Best channels for my content marketing are:

_____

_____

I will use the following content marketing strategies:

1.

2.

3.

4.

5.

6.

7.

MEET CONCLUSIONS

What barriers should I overcome to meeting people?

What new products or services do I have in the works that require a launch?

Does my audience view me as the expert and where can I showcase my expertise?

REMIND

After this step, you will have invited your customer into your experience and provided solutions to bring them one step closer to purchasing.

In the Remind phase, you will build or modify your Press Release, Consultation or Service Model and your Packaged Deals. Leverage the feedback from your Market Survey and Know Your market information as input.

Instructions:

1. Fill in of the Press Release pages and use these to reach the Media.
2. Fill in your Consultation or Service Methodology.
3. Fill in your Packaged Deal information to develop product or service offereings.
4. Once you have collected your information, write your conclusions and use this as input to the Cement phase.

PRESS RELEASE

The key to a good press release is making it newsworthy. Advertising an upcoming sale of your products is not newsworthy. Writing about a problem your market has and how that problem can be solved by your product is newsworthy. Other reasons to write a press release include: an announcement of the grand opening of a business; an upcoming open house; a product launch or some other new release; an announcement of an award received; and upcoming special events. (**See Pages 79 - 84 - Plans to Prosper: Strategies, Systems and Tools for Small Business Marketing Success paperback book**)

Newsworthy topics on which I can submit a press release are:

1.

2.

3.

4.

5.

6.

7.

The local news outlets in my area and the contact information is:

_____

_____

_____

_____

The agency or copywriter I will leverage is?

_____

_____

Timeline for submitting press releases for this quarter are:

_____

_____

_____

Press Release Template:

FOR IMMEDIATE RELEASE:

[Headline]

[Subhead – not required]

[Location & Date] – [News Article]

END

# # #

[Company Contact Information]

The media outlets that picked up my press releases are:

_____

_____

_____

CONSULTATION MEETING AS A MARKETING TOOL

(See Pages 85 - 90 - Plans to Prosper: Strategies, Systems and Tools for Small Business Marketing Success paperback book)

Lead generation ideas that would be of value to my market are:

1.

2.

3.

4.

5.

6.

7.

What consultation meeting can I offer my prospects to see if there is a match between their needs and my product or service?

_____

_____

_____

The name of my consultation is: _____

The benefits and takeaways for my prospect from my consultation are:

_____

_____

The retail price for this consultation is: _____

Use a CRM like Honor Services Office to create a sign-up form for your website.

What does the Consultation Meeting look like for a product?

    Set – Up?

    Demonstration

    Special Features

    Taste Test (Food Industry)

    Expansion Capabilities (Retail)

What does the Consultation Meeting look like for a service?

    Challenge Identification

    Desired outcome

    Plan Development

Follow-up steps after a consultation for prospects that do not convert are:

    1.

    2.

    3.

    4.

    5.

    6.

    7.

8.

9.

Track the number of consultations requested, booked, and closed in your key business metrics each month.

PACKAGED DEALS

What products / services can I pull together to provide a packaged deal that will give my prospects the result they desire? (**See Pages 91 - 94 - Plans to Prosper: Strategies, Systems and Tools for Small Business Marketing Success paperback book**)

_____

_____

_____

Consider:

- Can I bundle together items that are slow sellers with hot sellers?

- Can I bundle inexpensive services together to form a profitable service package?

- Is my packaged deal flexible?

- Can I repackage my product or service to provide a mini-solution?

Profit Calculator:

	Item 1:	Price:
Slow Mover	Item 2:	Price:
	Item 3:	Price:
	Total	_____

Mark Down

What testimonials do I have that speak to the results and benefits my prospects want from my product or service?

_____

_____

What technology will I use to sell the solution?

_____

_____

What will help to reduce the risk of saying yes to my packaged deal, product or services? E.g. Money back guarantee, trial period, refund of unused portion, etc.

_____

_____

_____

Track the number of packaged deals sold and measure the success in your key business metrics each month.

REMIND CONCLUSIONS

What newsworthy events can I be part of to keep my audience ignited?

What events can I be part of to mention my consultation?

What products or service should I eliminate versus bundling?

CEMENT

After you complete this step, you will solidify the relationship with your customer base and your role as the expert.

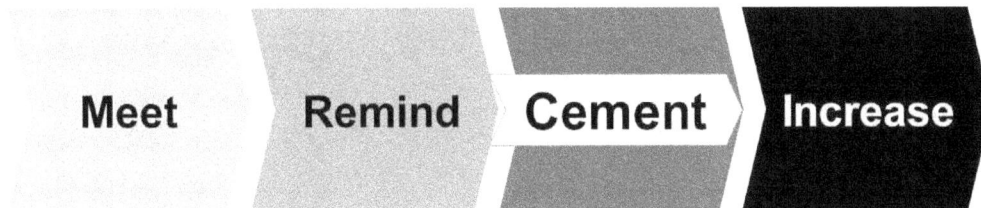

In the Cement phase, you will develop your Newsletter and email Marketing Strategy. Here you will want to think strategically not noisy.

Instructions:

1. Fill in of the Newsletter Strategic Plan.
2. Fill in your Email Marketing Strategic Plan
3. Once you have collected your information, write your conclusions and use this as input to the Increase phase.

NEWSLETTER

(See Pages 96 - 98 - Plans to Prosper: Strategies, Systems and Tools for Small Business Marketing Success paperback book)

What is the purpose of my newsletter?

_____

_____

What relevance cycle will I use versus a date?

_____

_____

What information will be of interest to my readers? NOTE: Look back at what was written in the Content Marketing section.

_____

_____

Do I have a set of pictures I can share?

_____

_____

What product or service information can I include in my newsletter? (Only 20% or Less of all newsletter content)

_____

_____

What calls to action can I use in my newsletter (other than buy this product or service)?

_____

_____

Track the articles read by my followers and the click through rates to measure success.

EMAIL MARKETING CAMPAIGNS

(See Pages 99 - 103 - Plans to Prosper: Strategies, Systems and Tools for Small Business Marketing Success paperback book)

What is the primary message of my email marketing campaign?

_____

_____

What compelling words can I use to enable a higher open rate? What would be appealing to by target audience?

_____

_____

What picture can I use to explain what I am selling? Is my message 80% Picture and 20% words?

_____

_____

What is my Call to Action?

_____

_____

What groups can I separate my list into? (Should I separate the list by Industry or city or something else?)

_____

_____

Has my list "Opted In"? Are all of the emails on my list still relevant?

_____

_____

What are my Open Rate, Click-Thru Rate expectations?

_____

_____

Have I done a search on spam words to avoid?

_____

_____

Can I make my email picture look professional or should I outsource this?

CEMENT CONCLUSIONS

How has the Newsletter affected my Marketing Calendar ?

How has the Email Marketing Strategy affected my overall Marketing Plan?

Is my messaging consistent with Content Marketing and my mission?

INCREASE

After this step, you will have prepared the items to increase the awareness, visibility, and loyalty of your customer base.

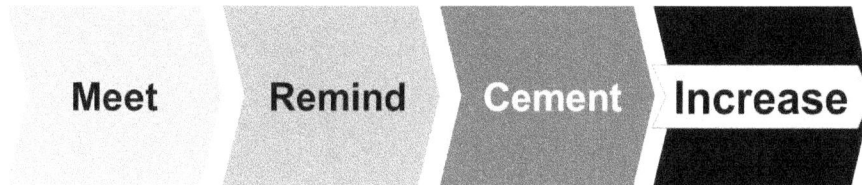

In the Increase phase, you will develop your Social Media Business Pages. These should be done professionally so people will want to connect with you and follow your business. . Advertising can be expensive so leverage the Advertising section to maximize your dollar.

Instructions:

1. Fill in of the Social Media Strategic Plan pages.
2. Fill in your Advertising Strategic Plan
3. Once you have collected your information, write your conclusions and use this as input to the Third 30 Days - Follow Up Phase.

SOCIAL MEDIA BUSINESS PAGES

(See Pages 105 - 109 - Plans to Prosper: Strategies, Systems and Tools for Small Business Marketing Success paperback book)

Facebook and Google+

What do my Facebook & Google+ Business page look like?

_____

_____

What is the purpose of my Facebook & Google+ pages?

_____

_____

Would a business page or group page be a better way for my market to engage with me and my business?

_____

_____

I will measure the success of my Facebook & Google+ pages the following ways:

1.

2.

3.

4.

5.

Changes/Additions to my Facebook & Google+ pages I will make this quarter are:

_____

_____

LinkedIn

What does my LinkedIn Business page look like?

_____

_____

Is my business page tied to a discussion group?

_____

_____

What is the purpose of my LinkedIn page?

_____

_____

Changes/Additions to my LinkedIn page I will make this quarter are:

_____

Twitter

What does my Twitter page look like?

_____

_____

What is the purpose of my Twitter profile?

_____

_____

Changes/Additions to my Twitter profile and account this quarter are:

_____

_____

Video

What video do I have of my product or service?

_____

_____

Is the video 2 minutes or less?

What other videos would be beneficial to my prospects and position me as an expert or leader in my industry?

_____

_____

I will setup my YouTube channel by: _____

Affiliates

What affiliates can I share on my page?

_____

_____

ADVERTISING

(See Pages 110 - 114 - Plans to Prosper: Strategies, Systems and Tools for Small Business Marketing Success paperback book)

What are my advertising expectations?

_____

_____

How many people must I reach in order to justify the capture rate?

_____

_____

What is my call to action?

_____

_____

Where will I advertise?

_____

_____

How will I measure the effectiveness of my ad?

    Online Metrics

        Click-Thru

        Impression

Location

Where will I advertise?

_____

_____

Content

Write your 40 word ad here:

_____

_____

_____

_____

_____

_____

Write your 20 word ad here:

_____

_____

_____

_____

Write your 15 word ad here:

_____

_____

_____

Write your 10 word ad here:

_____

_____

What is my advertisement budget? (2 – 7% of your gross sales)

_____

_____

INCREASE CONCLUSIONS

How has your Social Media Business Pages affected your Marketing Calendar?

How has Advertising affected your Marketing Budget?

Have I considered advertising in free places and other connection's Business Pages??

SECOND 30 DAYS IMPLEMENTATION CHECKLIST

Meet

☐ Read the Second 30 Days section to get an overview.

☐ Identify two or three places to network and meet prospects, power partners, and peers.

☐ Create a strong follow-up process for after networking to build relationships.

☐ If opening a new business or launching a new product or service, decide on how to announce it.

☐ Create a plan and follow up for next launch using multiple strategies.

Remind

☐ Make a list of four or five newsworthy topics on which to submit press releases.

☐ Identify local and/or national news outlets and contact information for submitting your press releases.

☐ Write (or have written) a press release and submit it.

☐ Create a list of topics for content marketing pieces.

☐ Plan a publishing schedule for upcoming content marketing, social media and press releases.

☐ Brainstorm lead generation ideas of value to your ideal market.

☐ Decide what kind of consultation to offer and outline the benefits and takeaways for the prospect.

☐ Outline consultation follow-up process.

☐ Review top five challenges of your ideal market and create a program or packaged deals to solve the ideal market's problems.

☐ Draft a lead generation tool.

☐ Add consultation name and takeaways to website.

Cement

☐ Select a client relationship management tool for tracking contacts and sending a newsletter.

☐ Decide the frequency for a newsletter.

☐ Create a newsletter template.

☐ Compile a newsletter with thought-provoking pictures, relevant information, and calls to action.

Increase

☐ Select one or two content marketing channels the ideal market uses to share the content.

☐ Set up complete profiles on the selected social media platforms.

☐ Decide if advertising is the right strategy for reaching the market and create a budget.

☐ Have a professional ad created if applicable.

THIRD 30 DAYS—FOLLOW-UP PHASE

Retain   Assess   Modify   Close

RETAIN

After completing this step, you will have the tools in place to keep your market coming back for more and sending others your way.

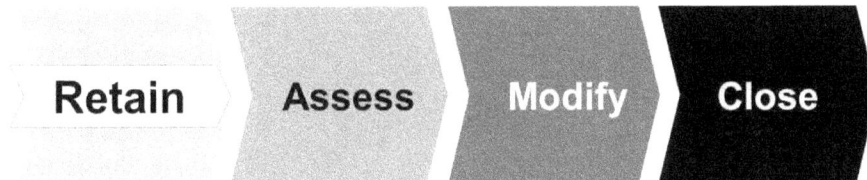

In the Retain phase, you will develop your Follow Up, Loyalty and Referral Strategies. This will determine how often people will return back to your business..

Instructions:

1. Fill in of the Follow Up pages and determine how you will keep in touch with your entire base of people.
2. Fill in your Loyalty Strategic Plan and keep it simple if you have not done this before.
3. Once you have collected your information, write your conclusions and use this as input to the Assess Phase.

FOLLOW-UP

(See Pages 121 - 123 - Plans to Prosper: Strategies, Systems and Tools for Small Business Marketing Success paperback book)

My follow-up process is:

1.

2.

3.

4.

5.

6.

7.

8.

9.

Use a CRM that has a reminder and auto-responder to tell you when to follow-up and automate part of the process.

What is your reminder speech?

How often will you reach out?

What content can you provide on the follow-up to show your expertise?

Select key performance indicators to track and assess marketing success or areas of improvement.

LOYALTY AND REFERRAL PROGRAMS

Once you have taken the time to acquire and convert a client, it's important to take great care of them so they stick around. It is also less expensive to market to existing clients than it is to acquire a new one. **(See Pages 124 - 128 - Plans to Prosper: Strategies, Systems and Tools for Small Business Marketing Success paperback book)**

The interval of purchases I wish to reward and around which to create my loyalty program is:

_____

_____

Start small with your loyalty and referral program and increase the size annually.

The loyalty rewards and referral incentives I will create that enable ROI are:

_____

_____

The kind of client communication vehicle(s) I will use, and at what intervals they will be sent:

_____

_____

What collateral will I use to help my clients track their referrals and loyalty rewards:

_____

_____

RETAIN CONCLUSIONS

What barriers will I face by not following up?

Should I perform another Market Study regarding my competitors Loyalty Programs?

What affect will Follow Up, Loyalty and Referral programs have on my overall Marketing Plan?

ASSESS

After completing this step, you will understand the key performance indicators from the metrics of your marketing campaign as input to making changes to your approach.

Retain ⟩ **Assess** ⟩ Modify ⟩ Close

In the Assess phase, you will review your overall marketing approach. Look at setbacks (if any) and determine your adjustments. Review all metrics to see how you performed against your goals..

Instructions:

1. Fill in of the Dealing with Marketing Setbacks pages and determine how you will adjust.
2. Fill in your Marketing Metrics in the Tracking Metrics form.
3. Once you have collected your information, write your conclusions and use this as input to the Modify Phase.

DEALING WITH MARKETING SETBACKS

When faced with a marketing setback, it is helpful to step back and look at the situation as objectively as possible. To do this, it may be helpful for you to ask yourself a series of questions including these:
(**See Pages 131 - 134 - Plans to Prosper: Strategies, Systems and Tools for Small Business Marketing Success paperback book**)

What has worked:

_____

_____

_____

_____

What are some of the positive results I have achieved?:

_____

_____

_____

_____

Did my message resonate with my audience?:

_____

_____

_____

_____

Did I target the right segment?:

_____

_____

_____

_____

Did I give this strategy enough time to really work?

_____

_____

What needs to be done for this marketing strategy, tactic or campaign to get better results?

_____

_____

_____

_____

_____

_____

DEALING WITH BAD REVIEWS

I will check my social reputation and reviews:

_____

_____

Ways in which I will respond to positive and negative reviews:

_____

_____

_____

_____

TRACKING AND METRICS

In your marketing plan, you set goals that you wanted to achieve by a certain date. Now, it is time to review these goals to see how your marketing efforts performed.
(See Pages 135 - 138 - Plans to Prosper: Strategies, Systems and Tools for Small Business Marketing Success paperback book

High-Achieving Marketing Process™ Step			
Meet	**Goal or Target**	**Actual**	**Difference**
• Marketing While Networking			
• Open for Business			
• Content Marketing			
Remind			
• Press Releases			
• Consultation as a Marketing Tool			
• Packaged Deals			
Cement			
• Newsletter			
• Email Marketing			
Increase			
• Social Media			
• Advertising			

ASSESS CONCLUSIONS

Did I attain my goals?

What did not go as planned?

How much time should I spend ?

MODIFY

After this step, you will have modified your marketing plan and made changes to the approaches you will use on the next marketing cycle.

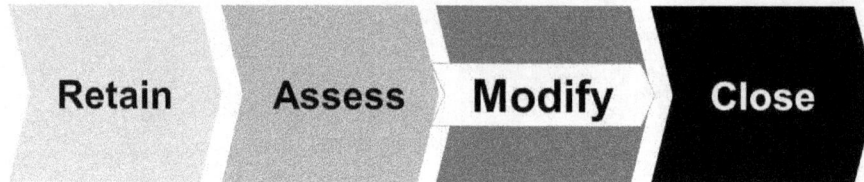

In the Modify phase, you will review your overall marketing approach and make adjustments to your approach and plan.

Instructions:

1. Modify your Marketing Plan once you have executed the entire strategy.
2. Once you have collected your information, write your conclusions and use this as input to the Close Phase.

MODIFY YOUR MARKETING APPROACH

(See Page 140 - 141 - Plans to Prosper: Strategies, Systems and Tools for Small Business Marketing Success paperback book)

Assess positive and negative metrics for the purpose of modifying your marketing approach. What patterns or observations have I made are:

_____

_____

Using my metrics as a baseline my next goals are:

_____

_____

_____

Tactics that have not been working that I will remove from my plan are:

_____

_____

_____

Subtle yet purposeful changes I can make to my approach are:

_____

_____

Ways I can challenge myself and business to be different are:

_____

_____

_____

_____

_____

CLOSE

After this step, you will have completed one full marketing cycle and are beginning to prepare for the next wave. Marketing is iterative and should be done for the life of your business.

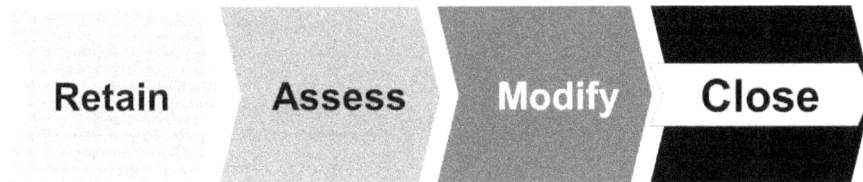

CLOSE THIS WAVE OF MARKETING

(See Pages 143 - 144 - Plans to Prosper: Strategies, Systems and Tools for Small Business Marketing Success paperback book)

What new or emerging markets can I serve?

_____

_____

_____

_____

Is it time to freshen up my product line or add additional service offerings? If so, what would that look like? How will it affect my brand?

_____

_____

_____

_____

Ways I can improve my message to my market are:

_____

_____

_____

_____

Ways I can improve my customer service are:

_____

_____

_____

_____

THIRD 30 DAYS IMPLEMENTATION CHECKLIST

Retain

- ☐ Identify the follow-up process for the selected lead generator(s).

- ☐ Develop a loyalty program.

- ☐ Develop a referral program with incentives of value to your customer base.

- ☐ Create a strong follow-up process to update our client base on what you are doing and what's new.

Assess

- ☐ Review what worked and what did not.

- ☐ Review your metrics.

- ☐ Give your marketing strategy enough time to work.

- ☐ Respond to reviews in a timely fashion.

- ☐ Add consultation name and takeaways to website.

Modify

- ☐ Ask your customers how they like your product or service for testimonials and feedback.

- ☐ Reestablish your goal based on performance metrics.

- ☐ Repackage your deal.

- ☐ Mix up your product offerings.

Close

☐ Check new and emerging markets.

☐ See if a product or service offering expansion is right for you.

☐ Assess your customer to see if you can reach a new demographic.

☐ Assess your message alignment with service.

☐ Believe in and start the High-Achieving Marketing Process.

☐ Target your market and have them fill out a survey to learn more about them.

CASE STUDY 1

This section is developed for your notes and is meant to be used with an accompanying presentation. Please follow the instructions given by your facilitator. In some instances you may be working in teams and some of the information may be recorded on supplemental sheets given to you.

Case Study Name: _____

Facilitator Name: _____

Facilitator Contact: _____

Team Name: _____

Team Member(s): _____

Team Member(s): _____

Team Member(s): _____

Contact Information: _____

Contact Information: _____

CASE STUDY 1 (BUSINESS PROBLEM)

Spend time by yourself or with your team to identify the business problem in the example given by your facilitator. Take good notes as you will be asked to report your findings.

_____

_____

_____

_____

_____

_____

_____

_____

_____

CASE STUDY 1 (ACTION STATEMENT)

Spend time by yourself or with your team to identify the action most suited to resolve this business issue in the example given by your facilitator. Take good notes as you will be asked to report your findings.

_____

_____

_____

_____

_____

_____

_____

_____

_____

CASE STUDY 1 (QUANTIFIABLE RESULTS STATEMENT)

Spend time by yourself or with your team to identify the quantifiable results (if any) you expect related to resolving this business issue in the example given by your facilitator. Take good notes as you will be asked to report your findings.

_____

_____

_____

_____

_____

_____

_____

_____

_____

CASE STUDY 2

This section is developed for your notes and is meant to be used with an accompanying presentation. Please follow the instructions given by your facilitator. In some instances you may be working in teams and some of the information may be recorded on supplemental sheets given to you.

Case Study Name: _____

Facilitator Name: _____

Facilitator Contact: _____

Team Name: _____

Team Member(s): _____

Team Member(s): _____

Team Member(s): _____

Contact Information: _____

Contact Information: _____

CASE STUDY 2 (BUSINESS PROBLEM)

Spend time by yourself or with your team to identify the business problem in the example given by your facilitator. Take good notes as you will be asked to report your findings.

_____

_____

_____

_____

_____

_____

_____

_____

CASE STUDY 2 (ACTION STATEMENT)

Spend time by yourself or with your team to identify the action most suited to resolve this business issue in the example given by your facilitator. Take good notes as you will be asked to report your findings.

_____

_____

_____

_____

_____

_____

_____

_____

CASE STUDY 2 (QUANTIFIABLE RESULTS STATEMENT)

Spend time by yourself or with your team to identify the quantifiable results (if any) you expect related to resolving this business issue in the example given by your facilitator. Take good notes as you will be asked to report your findings.

_____

_____

_____

_____

_____

_____

_____

_____

_____

CASE STUDY 3

This section is developed for your notes and is meant to be used with an accompanying presentation. Please follow the instructions given by your facilitator. In some instances you may be working in teams and some of the information may be recorded on supplemental sheets given to you.

Case Study Name: _____

Facilitator Name: _____

Facilitator Contact: _____

Team Name: _____

Team Member(s): _____

Team Member(s): _____

Team Member(s): _____

Contact Information: _____

Contact Information: _____

CASE STUDY 3 (BUSINESS PROBLEM)

Spend time by yourself or with your team to identify the business problem in the example given by your facilitator. Take good notes as you will be asked to report your findings.

_____

_____

_____

_____

_____

_____

_____

_____

_____

CASE STUDY 3 (ACTION STATEMENT)

Spend time by yourself or with your team to identify the action most suited to resolve this business issue in the example given by your facilitator. Take good notes as you will be asked to report your findings.

_____

_____

_____

_____

_____

_____

_____

_____

_____

CASE STUDY 3 (QUANTIFIABLE RESULTS STATEMENT)

Spend time by yourself or with your team to identify the quantifiable results (if any) you expect related to resolving this business issue in the example given by your facilitator. Take good notes as you will be asked to report your findings.

_____

_____

_____

_____

_____

_____

_____

_____

_____

ABOUT THE AUTHORS

Victoria Cook, founder and managing director for The Center for Guilt-Free Success, helps women entrepreneurs grow their businesses through coaching and training. Known for her proprietary 7-step Guilt-Free RESULTS™ process, Victoria often is in demand as a speaker. She was named a "Business Brick Builder" by the International Coach Federation Chicago Chapter in 2013. Her innovative approach reflects her commitment to building the strengths of her clients as she helps them market their businesses more confidently and easily.

Facebook: Ctr4GFSuccess

Twitter: Ctr4GFSuccess

www.centerforguiltfreesuccess.com

Stan Washington, a McDonald's executive turned entrepreneur is founder and president of Honor Services Office, software that helps small business grow sales, market businesses, and process invoices easily. He has helped thousands of small businesses achieve sales into the millions. His leadership of operations and technology enabled multi-billion dollar corporations to increase sales and he is ready to share their tips. Stan also is the co-author of Peaceful Selling: Easy Sales Techniques to Grow Your Small Business.

Facebook: HonorServicesOffice

LinkedIn: HSO Small Business Innovators

Twitter: KunakaNotes

www.HonorServicesOffice.com

Victoria and Stan met while serving on a local board of the International Coach Federation, an organization with 22,000 members. After discovering they shared a similar approach and mindset to marketing, they became passionate about working together to create a tool business owners like you could use to save money and grow a business simultaneously. The result is this resource.

OTHER DO IT YOURSELF RESOURCES

We truly hope you enjoyed this cross reference workbook. If you leveraged a facilitator then you will have the case study information that is not listed in this book.

Here are some other resources you can leverage to help grow your business:

Marketing Growth Tools

Plans to Prosper: Strategies, Systems and Tools for Small Business Marketing Success (Victoria Cook and Stan Washington) Copyright 2015 ISBN: 978-0-9909831-0-1

How to Create a Killer Elevator Speech eBook visit <ins>http://bit.ly/gf-kes</ins> and use promo code: plans2prosper to save 25% on your purchase.

30 Day Business Challenge register for a 30 day e-cource that provides a step-by-step process to reach YOUR big goals and provide daily action steps & inspiration to help you get there. Visit <ins>www.30DayBusinessChallenge.com</ins> and use promo code: plans2prosper to receive your discount.

Sales Growth Tools

Peaceful Selling: Easy Sales Techniques to grow Your Small Business (Dan Duster and Stan Washington) Copyright 2015 ISBN: 978-0-9909831-1-8

Peaceful Selling: Easy Sales Techniques Workbook (Dan Duster and Stan Washington) Copyright 2015 ISBN: 978-0-9909831-5-6

Business Management Software

Honor Services Office is a small business management tool that provides an easy to use CRM, Online invoice / Bookkeeping System and email Marketing system.

Visit <ins>http://www.HonorServicesOffice.com</ins> and use promo code: plans2prosper to receive your discount.